Totally
Committed

"TILL DEATH US DO PART"

"When things get hard, you don't leave. Staying revealed to me a deeper love than I'd ever known for my wife, Gail."

Timothy E. Lawrence

CITI OF
BOOKS

CITIOFBOOKS, INC.
3736 Eubank NE Suite A1
Albuquerque, NM 87111-3579
www.citiofbooks.com
Hotline: 1 (877) 389-2759
Fax: 1 (505) 930-7244

Ordering Information:
Quantity sales. Special discounts are available on quantity purchases by corporations, associations, and others. For details, contact the publisher at the address above.

Printed in the United States of America.

ISBN-13:	Softcover	979-8-89391-780-2
	eBook	979-8-89391-781-9

Library of Congress Control Number: 2025913432

Table of Contents

ACKNOWLEDGMENTS

First and foremost, I would like to thank my Lord and Savior, Jesus Christ, for giving me the strength and knowledge to write this book, and for helping me reach back into my memory to bring forth some of those things that might be of use to someone else reading it one day.

This book was written in memory of Gail Lynne Staten Lawrence, and dedicated to her three children: Darius C. Fentress, Brian P. Fentress, and Richard G.T. Lawrence. It is also dedicated to her parents, the honorable Bishop Gaston and Mrs. Lavern Staten, Sr., and the entire Staten family.

I would like to thank my wife, Maxine Lawrence, for her patience while I was writing this book. And I would also like to dedicate this book to all my children: Adam, Kelly Lance, Darius, Brian, Richard G.T, Richard Jr., Crystal, Joyya, and Emmanuel. I dedicate it as well to all my brothers and sisters: Charlene (now deceased), Richard (now deceased), Martha, David, Paul, Ruth, Carol, Jeanette, Jonathan, and James. And I dedicate it to all the Staten children: Gaston Jr., Steve, Ron, Reggie, Keith, Kimberly, Valerie, Andrea, and Michael.

I want to thank my close friends for standing by me: Rodney Smith, Michael Montgomery, and Cecil Banks as well as Fred Hammond for training my three sons in the music industry. I want to lovingly acknowledge my father-in-law, Otis Ghant, and my pastor and his wife, Melvin and Barbara Bailey. I thank my bishop, the honorable Curtis E. and Dr. Eleanor Montgomery, and I want to acknowledge my brother-in-law, Pastor Thomas R. Brown.

I want to thank my favorite and closest cousin/friend, who keeps me in stitches when I need it, the ever-lovin', no-one-like him, Mr. Anthony (Tony Too Tall) Dew. (I love ya, boy!) I also want to acknowledge my foster sister and brother who lived with my family since 1966: Elizabeth and Elisha Patterson. And I want to acknowledge my grandmother,

Natalie Lawrence, who always encouraged me, and my dear friend, Pastor Elbert Mondaine, who always called me his brother because we were born on the same day. Thanks!

Finally, I want to acknowledge my mother and step-father, the honorable Bishop Nealon and Mary Lawrence Guthrie, who encouraged me to keep the faith and who stood by me throughout this entire ordeal. Thank you for your genuine love, concern, and assistance. I would also like to acknowledge my deceased father, District Elder Richard E. Lawrence, whose example of being a loving husband and father inspired me to be a devoted and totally committed husband and father.

To The Reader

This book depicts my personal experience in caring for a disabled loved one. It is my hope that you will find, here, some valuable advice and/or encouragement to help you through a similar situation if it should ever happen to you. Too often well-meaning people make decisions for disabled loved ones that can then cause chaos and confusion within families. This happens primarily when they do not take time to find out what their loved one's needs are before the ability to communicate ceases. So take time to find out just what your loved one's final wishes are before it is too late, and then get a written directive as well. It will save everyone a lot of deep heartache and confusion in the long run.

CHAPTER 1
IN THE BEGINNING

Never in my wildest dreams did I think that, once married, everything would turn into a living nightmare.

I'd met Gail, my wife-to-be, through my aunt and uncle, who had flown out from Detroit to visit our family in Portland, Oregon, shortly before my brother was killed in a car accident. Indeed, the year 1985 proved to be an extremely difficult one for our family. Within a 12- month span of time, I lost my uncle, grandfather, great grandmother, oldest brother, and father - all under separate circumstances. That year could be a book in itself! But perhaps it helped prepare me for what was to come. At the time of my aunt and uncle's visit, though, I had no inkling there was yet more tragedy ahead.

Instead, my well-meaning aunt showed me a photograph of her sister's family, consisting of ten children. I found that interesting because my own family of origin had eleven kids big families both, in this day and age. The similarities between the two families were striking. They all sang, as did we, and their father was the pastor of their church, as was ours. Not only that, but their father was blind in his right eye, as was my own dad. It all seemed just too coincidental. Nevertheless, I saw Gail in that photo and immediately asked my aunt, "Who's that?" There was something about her that really grabbed my attention, so I got my aunt to tell me a little about her background.

Turns out Gail had been divorced for six years and had yet to go on a date. She'd evidently been with an abusive husband and wasn't too eager to risk her heart again. As soon as I saw her photo, though, I told myself that she would be my wife - just like my dad had said when he'd seen my mom's photo the first time. Well, when my aunt and uncle returned home to Detroit, my aunt evidently showed Gail a picture of me and teased her a little by saying I'd been asking lots of questions about her. Shortly after this, my brother was killed, and Gail unexpectedly sent me a sympathy card, which I found both surprising and sweet. I wrote back to thank her for the card, and one thing led to another. We started corresponding and then making phone calls, which led to a cross-country visit and our eventual engagement.

We married on July 12, 1986. I already had three children from a previous marriage who I had raised by myself. Gail had two children from her previous marriage as well. We were combining households and families and, at first, everything went surprisingly well. Gail was wonderful -- both as a wife to me and as a mother to all our children. She also managed the home perfectly, and we couldn't have been happier.

Within three months of our wedding she was already expecting what would be our sixth child - the first and only child born between us. Everything was going smoothly, and we were ecstatic about the impending birth. Even the pregnancy was going well - until that fateful day we decided to drive from Portland to Seattle to attend a friend's wedding.

Gail was about six months along when we made the easy, three-hour drive to Seattle. Upon arriving at the church, however, Gail took one step out of the car and discovered her right leg was dragging. We looked at each other, dumbfounded. "What's the matter?" I asked. "Why are you limping?"

She looked at me with a mixture of fear and dismay. "I don't know. I can't seem to move my right leg."

"What do you mean, you can't move it? Did it fall asleep on the way here?"

"No," she said. "It just refuses to work. I can't make it cooperate."

"Well, just hold on to me and we'll try it together," I said, moving to her side to act as a human crutch. It was slow going, but we finally made it into the church. Little did I realize that our clumsy trek across the parking lot that day would symbolize our years ahead: my wife clinging to me for support while her body failed her, our struggling in tandem to traverse what seemed an endless journey.

Of course, we both realized that something was definitely wrong and that Gail needed immediate medical attention. It wasn't just her pregnancy that was making it difficult to walk, and this was far more serious than just a pinched nerve. So, as soon as we returned home from the wedding, we began searching for doctors who could give us a diagnosis. It was surprisingly difficult to find anyone who could tell us what was going on with her body. We finally found a physician who agreed to take her case and whose research in this particular field of disease is world-renown. He diagnosed Gail as having Multiple Sclerosis.

At the time, we had no idea what "MS" was or what the implications of having it were. We were completely ignorant of the tumultuous road ahead that this cruel disease would lead us down. And it's just as well, I suppose. If I'd known then what I've since had to learn, I'm quite sure I would've given up before we even got started.

In practical terms, the first thing we had to do was buy Gail a cane so she could walk unassisted and keep her balance. Her leg didn't always "misbehave," as we came to call it. Sometimes it would work quite well but then suddenly give out on her at unexpected times or just hang useless for days or weeks on end. Thank goodness it didn't affect her pregnancy, though. A healthy baby boy was born to us three months later, on May 25, 1987. We found ourselves hoping that maybe things would just go back to normal after the baby was born and she had lost some of the weight she'd gained during her pregnancy. I mean, it's hard enough getting around when one is pregnant; perhaps Gail would miraculously improve after the baby came. But she didn't. Over the next few months it became increasingly difficult for Gail to walk - even with the cane.

From that point on, we were constantly seeking the best treatment for Gail we could find, which at the time included various pills and/ or injections, including steroid shots. Many of these treatments didn't work at all, though, and some worked only temporarily. It was highly discouraging, to say the least - and very expensive.

I was working ten and a half hours a day as a city bus driver just to keep food on the table and wondering the whole time when we would wake up from this nightmare. Little did I know that our sorrows were only beginning. The "Big Test" was still ahead, and I had to ask myself a hard question: Was I totally committed to taking care of someone with a disabling disease?

My first response to that self-imposed question was, "I sure hope so." I didn't know what to expect, and I kept wondering how long this difficult stage was going to last. We both hoped it would be over soon but, as we began to do further research on our own, we learned that part of what makes the disease of MS so unbearable is its unpredictability. It affects different people in different ways, as far as progression and disablement are concerned. Some of its effects can be severely crippling and ultimately fatal, while only minor symptoms ever surface for other patients. Some cases linger on for years, but other MS sufferers will go into what appears to be complete remission. Whatever the case, though, it is still a dreaded disease, and it takes its toll on both its victims and their caregivers.

Throughout the next two years, 1987-89, we somehow coped with Gail's increasing debilitation and made the necessary adjustments. Everywhere we went she had to be helped: in and out of cars, up and down stairs. When buying groceries, she relied on the shopping cart for walking stability, and it worked fairly well for a while. But by 1990 she was forced to start using a walker because it became increasingly difficult to maintain her balance. Indeed, all her motor skills were beginning to dissolve.

Little things, like just brushing her teeth or combing her hair even cooking dinner, became too hard for Gail to accomplish on her own. I eventually took over all the cooking, and our children got used to eating things "out of a box" or "out of a can." I just shake my head, now, at those trying days. It was a lot for all of us to get used to. Six children, the youngest of which was a rambunctious toddler, and their poor young mother tottering around with her own walker.... It was really stressful at times. But we must have done something right, for all of our kids are still around today.

Yes, to say it was difficult is an understatement. I was still working a demanding ten and a half hour shift driving bus, then had to come home and feed everybody, including my wife, who by then required spoon-feeding. No one can imagine how weary I was feeling. It's just as well we had no way of knowing that this relentless routine would span years. You just do the best you can each day, never realizing that each harried day quickly builds into weeks that become months and then years.

Sundays, Tuesdays, and Thursdays were the most trying days, though, because, in addition to the usual routine, we had the extra chore of preparing for church. Worshipping together as a family is essential in the face of struggles such as ours. So every Sunday morning I would wake everyone up in time to eat breakfast and dress for church. Not only did that mean cooking the breakfast myself and overseeing six energetic children, but I had to help my wife take her bath, get dressed, put on her makeup, style her hair, and then get everyone out the door in time for morning service. The same routine was repeated that night, for evening service, and then again on Tuesday and Thursday evenings. It was important for us, as a family, to faithfully attend church services, though, for it was only our faith in God that was getting us through.

By 1992, Gail traded in her walker for a wheelchair, and it seemed like everything began to go downhill from there. For the first time I began to really question why all this was happening to me - to us. What had I done to deserve this? My life had become so unbearably grueling; what was the purpose of this bleak existence? Every time I was tempted to feel sorry for myself, though, I would look at my poor wife and feel even sorrier for her. Why did she have to endure such misery and disablement? It was as difficult for her to adjust to her increasingly disabled body as it was for me to adjust to the extra workload. We were both exhausted and dismayed.

Our research showed that MS is stored in the fatty tissues of the body, so Gail had to resort to eating fat-free foods. At times her vision was impaired as well, although it would mysteriously come back for a short while. Sometimes she would lose it altogether, and we never knew just when that loss would become permanent. That was one of the most difficult parts of coping with this disease, I think: its unpredictability. There would always be just enough "turn arounds" to give us hope. But then that hope would be cruelly dashed only a few days or weeks or even months later, when the disability returned in full force. We were constantly making lifestyle adjustments, and the stress of never knowing what would "go wrong next" was taking its toll - as were the mounting medical bills and expenses. Things Gail normally did for herself increasingly had to be done for her. I could only imagine how that must have made her feel. I'm sure you would agree that such a situation would be difficult for anyone to handle.

But it did force me to do a lot of soul-searching. Would I (could !!) stick around and show her I am the man she thought I was? Or would I succumb to the temptation to just turn my back on our wedding vows - that holy promise to stand by her in sickness and in health and leave? One thing is for sure: You never know how life is going to turn out. We had to take it one day at a time because there was nothing else we could do.

We began looking for someone who could help us make it through each day. We found private caretakers to come in and assist us, but most of them didn't last long because they felt it wasn't worth what we could afford to pay. After much prayer, we finally found a caregiver who was consistent and stayed around a long while - mostly because she was a member of our church and lived right across the street from our house. There was also another member of our congregation who wanted to help out in any way she could, and we knew we could always count on her in a pinch, even though she had a family of her own and worked graveyard shift. Indeed, we were so very grateful for Flora McCray! I will never forget her generous spirit. She would often come over right after her shift ended just so she could help out. She did it out of love, with no expectation of monetary return.

For those of you who may be facing a similar situation with a loved one who is incapacitated, it is important to find a close friend or relative who can occasionally relieve you so you can take a break. Otherwise, you become so overly stressed and exhausted that your own health is in danger. We truly never would've made it through this horrendous ordeal without the assistance of various "God-sends" - people like Flora who were willing to pitch in and help carry our overwhelming load. God bless them all!

CHAPTER 2
MAKING THE CHANGE

While my wife's body was in transition, our house underwent its own kind of transition. We had to add handrails to most every room and make things wheelchair accessible wherever we could. I went through my own transitions as well: I had to learn how to apply Gail's make-up, mainly by trail and error, and there were quite a few times we would get to laughing at my clumsy efforts. It was a real chore at first, but I eventually got the hang of it and actually became quite good. My friends used to tease me that I could open a beauty salon.

Doing Gail's hair was a whole other story, though. I had to learn how to roll her hair up in curlers and then try to style it afterwards. This was much more challenging than doing make up, even though I eventually got the knack of it. But the greatest trial was dealing with pantyhose. Whoever designed those things sure never had to put them on someone else! I was always pulling and ripping or pulling and snagging them. I must have gone through at least three pairs of pantyhose a week - even after I got the hang out it! It wasn't getting them on that was the problem: it was doing so without incident, keeping them intact.

One day someone told me about "thigh-high hosiery" and I was baffled. "What on earth is that?" I asked. They told me they were nylons that you put on each leg, separately, and I decided right then and there that this person (not to mention the makers of such an ingenious device) was a God-send. What a huge difference such a small matter can make in the lives of disabled persons and those who assist them! It was important to my wife and her rapidly diminishing self-esteem to look as presentable as possible, and I did everything I could to help her in that area. Just a small thing like looking pretty, even while sitting in a wheelchair (especially while sitting in a wheelchair!) was so very important to keeping her spirits up and making her feel less disabled.

Sometimes we take for granted how easily we walk, talk, gesture, and move our limbs. But when one of those limbs suddenly stops working, we panic because we are so used to them automatically performing what we ask. Indeed, we don't even have to "ask." They just do it in response to an unconscious thought. But with MS, the body begins to "ignore" the brain's signals. The limbs just stop working, then the interior muscles, and there's nothing that can really be done about it.

As one might imagine, such a "betrayal" of one's body can have a deep impact on a person's mental and emotional health. When Gail was first diagnosed with MS, she was scared, just like anybody would be. We were all praying, of course, that it would just miraculously go away. But, as fate would have it, the disease progressed and she eventually grew to accept it, doing her best to deal with her deteriorating body. She did grow frustrated and impatient at times, of course - just like anyone would. But she rarely complained through the entire ordeal, saying instead that, "God must have a reason for me to go through this." That kind of faith-filled attitude really helped her to cope, I think. And it made it difficult for me to complain about my own aches and pains! Her bravery was inspiring, and I was challenged to do all I could to assist her in coping with the trial her body had become.

One of the many changes we had to adapt to was Gail's failing circulation. Her legs would be cold much of the time and she began losing feeling in her lower extremities. Consequently, her abdominal muscles lacked the strength to push during bowel movements, preventing her body from eliminating waste. After trying every possible pill and liquid stool softener and/or laxative available, I finally had to reach up into her rectum by hand and dig out the waste. It wasn't pleasant for either of us, to say the least, but it had to be done, and quite often.

Along with that uncomfortable procedure, I also had to catheterize her at least three or four times a day so she could urinate. Each of these procedures required that I physically lift her onto a bed or into a reclining chair so she could receive treatment. It was exhausting for both of us, to be sure, and made even more unbearable by the overload of medications she was taking.

Because Gail was taking so many different kinds of prescription drugs by this point, she no longer felt like herself. The meds began to counteract with each other, and it just became too much for her system to bear. She began having severe mood swings and behaving in ugly ways that weren't like her at all. I knew something was going on, so I called the doctor and explained the situation. He had us cut back on a certain medicine and she immediately began to mellow out, becoming more like her usual self.

Even from her wheelchair, though, Gail continued to rule the house like nothing was wrong. I used to call her "Iron Sides" because, when it came to doing things she wanted to do, nothing would stop her. When things looked like they wouldn't turn out the way she wanted, she would persist until they did. Perhaps it was because she had so little control over her body, now, but she managed to control circumstances and situations in a truly remarkable way. Her body may have been weak, but her spirit was still domineering!

For example, one day we had only one loaf of bread left in the house, and she had wanted to make sandwiches from it. But, while putting them together, the whole thing fell on the floor. "Pick it up," she laughingly ordered. "Sandwiches WILL be made!"

Another time Gail was shopping in a clothing store when her uncooperative bladder decided to "leak." "Honey," I said, shouldn't we go take care of that?"

"Nope. I'm not done shopping yet," she proclaimed, refusing to be thwarted by such a minor inconvenience. She was determined to let nothing stop her from what she wanted to do, as much as it was in her power to do so.

Perhaps the most memorable example of Gail's determination to keep living as though she were "normal," though, came when our entire family decided to take a much-needed vacation to Six Flags amusement park in Los Angeles, shortly after Gail had been confined to a wheelchair.

She wasn't about to miss out on the fun just because of this latest "lifestyle change" and insisted on going on "Top Gun," one of the scariest rides there. Indeed, I was even too scared to go on it! We lifted her up into the seat, the attendants strapped her in, and away she went. It raced up and down, looping wildly over and around some water, causing everyone to scream. But as soon as the ride was over, she wanted to do it again. She loved it!

For a while we managed to hire a physical therapist who came in at least once a week to help Gail with her range of motion. But the young woman chose to quit when she got married and then never returned. This was deeply disappointing to Gail, of course, and she began rapidly declining after that. Exercise is critical for people with MS because it helps the body stay strong, and the stronger one is the better able he or she is at coping with this insidious disease. We tried and tried to find another therapist who would come help Gail, but by then we couldn't afford one.

This was the other devastating part of struggling with a disease like MS that few talk about: the astronomical expenses! Not only must you endure the constant changes in your body that then necessitate changes in your lifestyle and living conditions, but the accumulating bills (both medical and non-medical) become a huge financial drain. Much to our dismay, we ended up having to eventually file bankruptcy. Indeed, I lost most everything I possessed before this nightmarish ordeal was over.

It was truly a paralyzing position to find myself in. I couldn't possibly work any more hours than I already did, and whenever I wasn't at home we had to hire someone to care for Gail and the kids or else rely on the generosity of friends and fellow church members, which we did a lot. But the expenses just kept adding up, even with insurance, and no matter how hard I worked, we couldn't reduce that ever-increasing mountain of debt. Between the caregivers, the special foods, the medicines, the personal items she needed, plus nursing costs and medical bills, it all grew into a mountain I just couldn't climb.

At the time of our marriage, back in 1986, my credit rating was excellent. I had a good position as a city bus driver and could easily afford my new wife and family of six. I also had a large selection of credit cards, some of which had $15,000 credit limits. After Gail's health began to deteriorate, though, I began using those credit cards in a desperate attempt to buy her the help she needed. I managed to eventually max out all those cards, and even spent the $25,000 I had stashed away through the company's deferred compensation savings plan. Not only was it difficult to keep up with these mounting bills, but it was impossible even to find the time to deal with them! My daily routine was exhausting, to say the least. No matter how many times I had to get up to help my wife use the bathroom during the night (and then clean her up afterwards when her "aim" was off), I still had to get up at 5:20 A.M. in order to arrive at work by 6:20 A.M. During that one hour of morning preparation time, and in addition to getting myself ready for the day, I had to get Gail up and catheterize her, carry her downstairs to the lower bedroom, and then leave her there until the caregiver arrived, at least two hours later. Thank goodness, though, the children were still getting ready for school, so she was never left alone in the house. But our routine wasn't healthy for any of us. I was only averaging three to five hours of sleep per night - and that's not nearly enough for someone who drives a city bus for a living! As soon as my shift ended, I'd rush home to relieve the caregiver, and then cook dinner and make sure everybody got fed. After dinner, Gail enjoyed watching her favorite TV show, "Jeopardy." She always sat in the big lounge chair, watching television, or she would help the children with their homework. After a few hours, during which time I washed the dishes and cleaned up as best I could, it would be time for bed and I had to reverse the morning's process: roll her hair up in curlers, take off her make-up, carry her into the bathroom to brush her teeth and wash her face, and then carry her back upstairs to our bedroom, where I laid her in bed and then catheterized her. If it was a church night (which happened two days a week), or a Sunday morning, the ritual of preparation had to be doubly repeated: get her up, catheterize her, do her hair, put on her make-up, dress her, feed her, and then get her into the car. From there we would drive to church, which didn't have a handicap ramp, so I would have to pull her wheelchair up the stairs backwards, into the sanctuary. When church service was over, we did the same thing in reverse to go home (where we didn't have a ramp either). And this routine was repeated for the next several years, until 1995, when Gail came down with pneumonia and had to be hospitalized. At this point, and because of her overall poor health, it became necessary to put Gail into a care facility after she was released from the hospital. The breakdown of my wife's body was finally too much for us to handle without full-time professional help. Up until then I had done all I could to keep from putting her into a care home, but after the pneumonia scare it was obvious that Gail needed twenty-four hour, 'round-the-clock nursing. I thought (mistakenly) that my "physical work" with her was now done. But, as anyone who has cared for a loved one in a nursing facility knows, there was still a lot of "caring" to do, even while paying someone else to supposedly do it. I visited her constantly, every day after work and on weekends. I kept her eyes cleared and her nose cleaned, and if her body hadn't been as well washed as either of us thought suitable, then I'd bathe her again myself. I also kept her fingernails and toenails manicured. When I look back at all I did over those years of increasingly demanding care, I can hardly believe it. How had I managed to do it all? It was so hard at times that anyone who has not been through it simply has no idea. To be honest, I would sometimes come home after spending an evening with her at the care home, slump down into my recliner, completely exhausted, and yet unable to relax for fear of wondering what new request for help might be waiting to pounce. I jumped every time the phone rang, thinking it was from the care facility, with news of some new problem that had arisen or some new need Gail now had. So even with her in the care home, I discovered I still couldn't rest. I felt always on alert, on "standby," never knowing when I'd be asked to get up and come help. It wasn't as bad as when she'd still been living at home, however. Indeed, I was so stressed out back then that one morning I woke up and my brain was literally buzzing like I'd stuck my finger in a socket. I realized I was on the verge of a nervous breakdown, so I quickly called the caregiver and asked her if she could stay with Gail and the children for a few days so I could get away. Thank goodness she said "yes." It was definitely time for a break! So I went to the coast for two and a half days by myself, just to rest. When I got back, I was fine; just a little time away, out from under all that responsibility, made all the difference in the world.

I realize now, first-hand, how extremely important it is for anyone caring for someone with a disability to find ways to alleviate the tremendous stress that builds up. It's impossible to calculate just how much pressure your own body is going through in response to always being on hand for someone else - until it just starts shutting down. Then you find yourself wondering, "What's wrong with my body?" You might be telling yourself that you're simply "tired." But what most of us don't realize is the tremendous wear and tear on our bodies that the pressure of caretaking exacts - in addition to the emotional toll, of course.

To be honest, there were times when I was just so incredibly weary of the whole thing, both emotionally and physically, that I wanted out. What made it especially (and unexpectedly) difficult, of course, were the temptations I faced from other women who wanted to "comfort" me. That was really hard to deal with! At times I just wanted to give in. But I would only let it get so far, and then something inside me would rise up and say, "No! I'm not going to do this." I remembered that I had made a promise to God that I would never sleep with another woman while I was married, and I managed to keep that promise, hard as it was at times. I am proud to be able to say, now, with God as my witness, that I was never unfaithful to my wife.

CHAPTER 3
"DON'T LEAVE ME HERE!"

If you ever plan on eventually admitting a loved one into a care center or nursing home, be prepared for an intensely emotional event. Trust me: Leaving someone you love and care about in a facility of any sort (against their wishes) will wreak havoc on your emotions. My sister-in-law and I tried to explain to my wife why we were leaving her there in the care center. But she was so upset, especially when we began to leave, that we could still hear her shouting behind us as we walked down the hallway: "Where are you going? Where am I? Don't leave me here! PLEASE DON'T LEAVE ME HERE!"

As her voice faded into a whimpering cry, she continued to plead, "Please, please, please don't leave me...."

Her sister and I were trying to hold it together, emotionally, as we left, but we just couldn't. We cried all the way out of the facility. It was truly the hardest thing I've ever had to go through in my entire life. But it had to be done. She needed full-time health care, and I couldn't give her that. I had done all I could do, for sure. But now the most loving, helpful thing I could do was ensure she received adequate around-the-clock nursing care. Leaving her there was an act of love, but she saw it as pure betrayal at the time. And knowing that she felt abandoned by me, her caretaker and best friend for the past nine years, felt more painful than a knife wound.

It took her about two weeks to adjust to being in the care facility. I visited her every day, no matter what -- unless I was sick, of course. Then I would call the care center to ask them to tell my wife why I was not going to make it that day. My new routine was physically easier in that I didn't have to get her up and ready for the day, but I still felt like her health (or lack of it, that is) dominated our lives. I still worked a full shift as a bus driver, came home to cook dinner and make sure everyone was fed, then visited Gail at the care center while my older children stayed home. My youngest would usually go with me, though. He was eight by the time we admitted her, and he got so he knew every employee at the facility. I always tried to bring him with me so he could be around his mother as much as possible. We'd stay there all evening whenever we could. But sometimes, on school nights, his older siblings would watch him while I went alone.

When I visited Gail without our son, I would always hang around until my wife drifted off to sleep, usually between midnight to 1:00 A.M. We would watch TV together, or I'd read to her. Although it was difficult for her to talk by then, we'd just try to communicate as best we could.

As time went on, her ability to eat and swallow diminished. One day I got excited to see she seemed to be swallowing everything she was eating, and I eagerly took it as a sign she might be improving. Not so. We discovered she was storing food in her cheeks because she could no longer swallow. At that point we were forced to make a critical decision. Should we give her a feeding tube or should we follow the written directive she'd earlier provided which stated she did not want life support of any kind?

I knew what Gail wanted, but I wasn't so sure her parents would agree with her decision. So I called them (they still lived in Detroit, Michigan) and told them everything that was going on. They were strongly opposed to my wife's decision to forego life-support, and they asked me to talk to her and see if I could get her to change her mind. I agreed to talk it over with Gail once more, but I assured them that it was her decision, after all. So I spoke with Gail as best I could, and she made it clear that she did not want the tube.

When I called her parents back to tell them of Gail's response, they pleaded with me to get her to change her mind. I felt incredibly torn, and finally agreed to try one more time to talk with her about it. This time I told my wife that her father was pleading with me to get her to change her mind and accept the feeding tube. After talking awhile, I got her to reluctantly agree to give in to her parents' wishes. A feeding tube was installed, and Gail's failing body was able to receive nourishment once more.

A few months later, though, the MS had progressed to the point that she lost all ability to speak, and verbal communication was impossible. We managed to establish communication via eye signals instead. Thankfully, we had planned our strategy before she lost her speech. One blink meant "yes;" two blinks meant "no." It worked quite well, despite the skepticism of some of her family members. They had trouble believing that she could really communicate that way. But communicate she did!

If you ever suspect a loved one (or yourself!) may be in danger of losing his or her ability to speak, you should agree upon and establish some sort of communication code in advance so you will be able to understand each other nonverbally. It is also a good idea to have a witness on hand as well, who understands the code you've agreed upon and who can then later help resolve any disputes that might arise with family members not familiar with your silent signals. It could certainly prevent a lot of headaches - not to mention animosity and suspicion by well-meaning family members who don't visit on a regular basis.

Every time I visited my wife I would immediately ask her how she was doing, despite the fact that she could no longer talk. "Are you all right? Are you cold? Are you hot? Are you uncomfortable?" I made sure I always asked questions that could be answered with a simple "yes" or "no." She would then communicate with me using eye-signals. Also, she would make certain sounds, like grunts or moans, letting me know if something was wrong. We had spent so much time together, long before she began to decline and then throughout her gradual deterioration, that I was fully adept at interpreting every little nuance of sound, gesture, or movement. Those who spend a lot of time with their loved ones, like I did with Gail, grow to understand these nonverbal signals intimately. This silent form of "intuitive" communication may be difficult for an outsider to grasp, thus leading to all kinds of misunderstandings later on. But this is why having an impartial "witness" to your agreed-upon nonverbal signals is so important.

It is also important to make sure that your loved one gets out of the facility as often as possible, up to several hours a day if he or she can handle it. It is hard on their spirits to be surrounded by the same four walls every day, day in and day out. Although many of them can no longer express their desire to be outdoors - or even in a different kind of environment, all you need to do is put yourself in their shoes for a while. What would you prefer?! While caring for Gail at the nursing facility, I saw and heard for myself every day how much even the most apparently "out of it" patients loved having a change of scenery. Just waiting for someone to pick them up the hope of change an outing of any kind implied - was enough to cheer their spirits. That is why it is so very important to be deeply compassionate with invalid loved ones. Because they are disabled and/or severely limited in their ability to communicate doesn't mean they have lost their ability to feel. Like us, they still have all their emotions intact, even though it has become difficult (sometimes impossible!) to express them. Indeed, their emotional state is usually even more fragile than is their caregiver's, and they often know what is being said about them even when it appears they don't. They just can't respond any longer.

The expense of committing Gail to a nursing facility really sent my already overwhelmed finances into a tailspin. I fell further and further behind on my bills and finally faced the humiliation of having one of my cars repossessed. (Thank goodness it wasn't working anyway, so it wasn't a huge loss.) But when my house went into foreclosure I was all but beside myself with anxiety. Where would I go, how could I ever afford another place? By then only my youngest son was left at home, so our household needs were less. But about this same time my supervisor told me I could not come back to work because I had sleep apnea. Although this is a treatable condition, it is considered a real liability for a bus driver, and they decided to retire me by way of permanent disability. Things felt like they couldn't get much worse....

I applied for social security disability, which I eventually got, but it came too late to save my house. I was forced to file bankruptcy and find a new place to live. Needless to say, by this time I was devastated, hurt, confused, dumfounded, and just plain old angry. I couldn't help wondering why all this was happening to me especially since I'd tried so hard to be faithful to both God and my wife through this whole ordeal. It just wasn't fair.

But God always provides a means of escape, especially when things are bleakest.

For quite awhile, now, Gail's parents had been suggesting that we move back east to live near them in Detroit. They were highly concerned about her health, of course, and wanted the chance to be near her. Since I was losing our home anyway, and my job was now ended, it seemed like the right time to make this big move. Although the deferred payment from social security plus the first of two disability checks came too late to save our house from foreclosure, they provided me with enough money to move Gail, our youngest son, and me back to Michigan where we could be near her relatives.

We arrived in Detroit the autumn of 1999 and found a nice nursing home in nearby Pontiac, about 15 miles away, for Gail to live in. Her family was overjoyed to have us move back there because they could now visit her any time they wanted to and they no longer had to fly 2700 miles across country to visit us in Portland, Oregon. I must admit we had a really good time living near her family in Detroit for the two and a half years we were there. I also have family in Detroit: aunts, uncles, and cousins. Being near family was important for both of us, and everyone was able to visit my wife as much as they liked. It really helped keep her spirits up, even though by this time her health had deteriorated to the point that she couldn't speak and cataracts had developed in her eyes to the point that she could barely see.

Thank goodness she was still able to recognize all the people who came to see her -- as long as they were standing right near her bed. Over time, though, her vision grew more and more cloudy, and it was mainly by our voices that she recognized us. It finally got to the point that, had it not been for my voice, she wouldn't have known when I was right in front of her. But she was happy to be near family again, and she seemed content, considering the circumstances. And there were certainly some rough circumstances!

Although we had looked hard and long to find the best possible care home for Gail when moving back there, I was horrified one day to discover Gail moaning in an unusual way. By then I knew her sounds so well that I could tell something was wrong. After closely inspecting her, I noticed that her foot, hidden under the covers, was swollen up the size of a basketball, and I immediately called over a nurse to find out what was wrong.

They seemed surprised, and although they tried to downplay it, her foot turned out to be broken. After much persistent questioning we learned that the attendant on duty a few nights before had dropped her while changing the sheets and hadn't bothered to report it. Needless to say, we immediately relocated her to another facility, and it was only a short while later that her previous "home" was shut down by the State.

Like I said earlier, even though your loved one is "safely" situated in a care home, it doesn't hurt to stay extra vigilant on his or her behalf. Sometimes those places just get so busy or short-handed that even important things get over-looked. Consequently, I all but lived in the nursing home with Gail, making sure to visit her every day. My new home in

Detroit wasn't far away, only about a 35-minute drive. And she had other family members coming to visit her as well, so she was well cared for. I realize this may sound strange, but somehow the worse Gail got the more I loved her. Caring for someone means loving them and wanting to do things for them and make them happy. My whole life revolved around caring for Gail, and my love for her just kept increasing.

I've often been asked if I had any indication that something was wrong with my wife even before I married her. The answer is an emphatic, "No, I did not!" Upon reflection, though, I suspect that both she and her family knew something wasn't quite right. I'm quite certain they didn't know what it was, but there had been little "red flags" indicating her body wasn't fully normal. For instance, prior to our wedding, Gail's brother also got married, and in order for Gail to walk down the aisle in the processional, they had to wrap one of her legs. During our courtship she would sometimes lose her balance, and I always thought she was just trying to be cute; she would always smile and play it off, as though just being silly. Little did I know these were signs something was wrong.

Likewise, my mother witnessed Gail losing her balance, back before we were married, when Gail was still living in Detroit. She didn't bother telling me about it until after we had wed and Gail began suffering obvious symptoms. But she said that she suspected something was wrong then but hadn't been able to put a finger on it. Only after the diagnosis did these little stories begin to leak out, filling in the larger picture.

For instance, it wasn't until after we learned about MS that my wife admitted the entire left side of her body had gone numb for about two weeks back when she was 17 years old. She said she hadn't known what was wrong and neither had the doctors. Of course, the medical community didn't know much about MS back in the 70's.

I've also been asked the unsettling question if I still would have married my wife if I had known she had MS.

Well, I've asked myself that question hundreds of times, and I must confess that, had I known what we would be facing, as well as the final outcome of the disease, I can say without any doubt that I would NOT have married her! Furthermore, I wouldn't want anybody to have to go through what we experienced. I truly believe that the average person could not have gone through what we did. It took an inordinate amount of dedication, love, and will power. The only other help I had besides that of caregivers and nurses was from my God in heaven. Truly, I had to have some kind of supernatural strength to physically lift dead weight up and down flights of stairs, day in and day out, for over eight years!

True, I did build up some muscle over time, which was a good side benefit from all that lifting, but this is not the sort of work a person can accomplish alone. Most of the time I had to face these challenges by myself, and believe you me, it was some kind of hard work! Looking back, I can't even imagine how I managed to work a ten and a half hour job only to come home to another ten and a half hours of caring for an invalid wife. And yet, that's what I did, with no time off on weekends. How did I do it, you may be asking. Well, by the grace of God and a lot of prayer from people all over the world who knew about our situation and graciously agreed to pray for us. Oh yes, and by being "totally committed." God honors those who honor Him!

Although our time in Michigan had been good for both of us, after about two and a half years or so, I felt it was time to move back to Oregon. I was getting homesick for my family there and wanted to visit my older children and have the opportunity of watching my grandkids grow up. Also, our Portland church desperately needed someone to play the organ, and that's one of the things I really enjoy doing.

However, when I announced our plans to move back west, my wife's parents became really upset. They demanded to know why I was taking their daughter away from them. I explained that it was time for us to return to my hometown now; they had gotten to enjoy their daughter being near them for the past two and a half years, and it was time for me (us!) to be near my children again, in Oregon. I had spent a lot of money relocating to Detroit so they could be near their daughter and everyone could be happy. But it was time for us to return to our "real" home now.

My explanations were useless, however. In fact, they even suggested I just return home without Gail and leave their daughter in Michigan with them. That response really hurt my feelings because I felt like they didn't care about me; they were only interested in their "little girl." Indeed, they were so upset that they even consulted a lawyer to see if I could be stopped. Now, I can understand why they didn't want her to go; after all, she was their oldest daughter and we all knew what her situation was. But, as her husband, I wasn't about to leave her behind, and I really felt compelled to return to Oregon. I wasn't trying to hurt them in any way, and I deeply respect them. But when it's time to go, it's time to go.

I explained it all to Gail, of course, and she indicated she understood what was going on. I don't think she really wanted to go, but she understood why I did and she didn't want to put up a fuss or prevent me from seeing my kids. There were other factors weighing on me, too, that I'd never told her parents about. For one thing, our apartment complex was getting ready to be turned into condos, and I didn't want to live anywhere else in Michigan except where we were: West Bloomfield. Also, my financial situation was getting tight again.

So, after much prayer and discussion, and to the great disappointment of Gail's parents, we moved back to Portland the summer of 2002, where we were gladly received. It was great being around our kids again, and the church was thrilled by our return. I was back home and loving it, and Gail seemed to have survived the move fairly well. But later that autumn her condition visibly declined and she just kept going downhill all winter. By the time spring came and everything was bursting with fresh growth, Gail's body had begun to shut down. I could tell her end was near.

CHAPTER 4
SHUTTING DOWN

E nd stage is hard to watch: every few weeks there is a change in mannerism or body language. Little things, like making Gail giggle or laugh, became a thing of the past. She was no longer responding in the ways we were used to seeing. I could tell she wanted to respond, but the disease wouldn't let her. I also knew she was still able to laugh inside, so I would continue saying things that I knew she would find funny - even though she couldn't express it outwardly. In fact, every day when I came to see her I would always try to come up with something silly to say to her in order to boost her spirits - and it most always worked.

Swallowing had become extremely difficult for her, and throughout the day I would watch her choke, just on her saliva. Sitting next to her as a helpless observer became increasingly difficult for me, too. It would make anybody cringe, I think, to witness her gagging, her body tightening up and becoming restricted, arms lifted slightly away from her body in the futile effort to get saliva down her throat. Because she's not ordinarily able to raise her arms, you know it's an intense moment for her. This "gagging" episode would happen every day, at least four or five times a day, and could not be controlled. Although it had been going on for several years now, by the spring of 2002 it was even worse.

One day I was sitting in her room visiting with her when I heard this unfamiliar sound coming from my wife. Remember how I said I knew her every whim? Well, this sound was different from what I was used to hearing. I looked at her and asked gently, "Is there something wrong, Tweety-Bird?" (That was the nickname I used to call her.) She cried out with this unusual whimpering I didn't recognize, and I kept asking, "What is it? What's wrong?" Then I began asking her a long string of "yes" and "no" questions, to detect what it was that might be bothering her. But she did not respond to any of them with a "yes" answer. I was confused because I was so used to knowing exactly what every little sound she made meant. Finally I said to myself, well, maybe she is trying to tell me she is tired of everything she has been going through. These sounds and emotions, if you were to look at her, made you think she was trying to say she was tired of living like this. She had blinked "no" to everything I had asked her so far, so I thought maybe I would ask the "Big Question."

"Honey, are you tired of living like this?"

It took her awhile to respond, but she finally blinked her eyes one time - our code for "yes."

I said, "What do you mean you are tired of living like this? You mean living with this disease?"

Again, she responded with one blink, "Yes."

I couldn't believe - or perhaps didn't want to accept - what she was telling me. I said, "Well, what do you want to do? I don't think we can do anything about it."

She then started whimpering, obviously distressed, so I said, "Okay, let me find out if there is something we can do about this matter."

I already knew there was nothing that could be done, of course, short of stopping her feeding tube -- which would of course end her life. And I also knew she wasn't going to say she wanted that, so I simply asked her, "Do you want to stop the feeding tube?"

To my amazement, she immediately blinked her eyes once, indicating "yes." I exclaimed, "Are you serious? Do you know what you're saying?"

I was scared, now, because that meant she would die. I asked her, "Do you know you will die if we remove the tube?" She again blinked her eyes one time, "Yes."

I got really scared then. It was apparent she really wanted to die. I couldn't believe it. So I ended up asking her, three separate times: "Are you sure this is what you want?" "Are you sure you are ready to die?" "Do you really want the feeding tube removed?"

She blinked her eyes "yes" three separate times, looking solemnly into my face. Again, I couldn't quite accept what she was "saying." So I said, "Don't you at least want to think about it?" She then blinked twice, meaning "no." Again, I asked, "Are you sure?" She blinked once: "Yes."

I told her, then, that I didn't want her to die yet, that I didn't want her to leave me. By now I was truly frightened. I mean, this was serious! She had just admitted to me she wanted to die!

So I told her, "I don't want you to go, but if this is what you really want, then I'll go talk to the head nurse and see what she can do."

I then tracked down the head nurse and repeated our entire conversation to her, telling her that my wife had decided she no longer wanted the feeding tube. She said she would of course have to confirm everything I said, and so she returned to my wife's bedside with me and asked her all the same questions - which Gail answered in exactly the same way, with no hesitation.

The nurse, like myself, now had no doubt as to what my wife really wanted, and she also knew what removing the feeding tube "meant." She quietly and simply asked me, "When do you want to start the procedure?"

At that point I kind of broke down, and said, "Please don't ask me that question, because I don't want to be the one to make that decision. Ask my wife. She will let you know."

So, on a Friday morning, the nurse asked my wife if she wanted to have her feeding tube pulled out the following Monday. And Gail indicated with one blink of her eyes, "Yes."

****

Monday, June 16, 2003: The tube feeding my wife and keeping her alive was removed. I'll never forget how peaceful her face looked once the tube had been taken out. Even the nurse commented on it. It's as though a huge struggle had finally been ended. I was concerned over what would happen next, of course.

"Will she feel any hunger pangs?" I asked the nurse. She replied that Gail would experience them for the first two days, but they would give her something to help with that and then the discomfort would go away altogether. Every day I would ask my wife, "Are you hungry? Do you want the feeding tube put back in?" And she would always blink her eyes, "No." I would say, "Are you sure?" And her eyes would signal, "Yes."

"You are so very brave," I told her, stroking her cheek, her hair. "I don't know if I could do this if I was in your shoes." The expression on her face caused me to suspect she was thinking, "If you had been through what I've had to endure all these years, I know you'd have made the same decision." And I like to think she was right.

I had been dreading telling Gail's parents about her choice, of course, but I reluctantly made that phone call a few days after the tube was pulled. They were very upset, to say the least, and they wanted to know who did it and why. I explained to them that this was their daughter's decision, but they could not accept that fact. They demanded to know why I hadn't called them first. I told them, "Because your daughter knew that you would try to talk her out of it."

By now I was upset, too, because it was obvious they still didn't trust my judgment. Despite all I had done for my wife and her (our!) children all these difficult years, here I was, getting verbally beaten up by them at the most critical point in our lives.

Once again, I didn't' know what to do. I felt hurt and confused; this was Gail's decision, not mine. I had simply asked the questions and she made the choices. Many of the family members came to visit Gail during those final days, but her parents did not. And I could never understand why. To this day, I still don't know how they really feel about me. But I do know they are people of integrity and that they don't hold grudges. I like to think they knew what great care I gave to their daughter over the years and how much I provided for her. So no matter how they view me, I will always love and respect them and their entire family.

Each day that went by after the feeding tube was pulled, Gail grew weaker and weaker. Her responses were becoming slower, and every day I would ask her again if she wanted the tube put back in. Despite her weakened body, though, she would muster what little strength she had left to blink her eyes two times, our signal for "no." It wasn't easy facing the end of Gail's life, knowing that death was inevitable and that she was drawing closer to it with each passing day. After so many years of struggling to survive and hang on, it seemed incomprehensible to just quit, give up. But that is what she was choosing to do, and her bravery in doing so seemed somehow as nobly determined as was her will to live.

It was certainly a very dramatic and sad situation, and I tried to be strong for her. But I realized that she was much stronger mentally and emotionally than I was. Watching the life drain right out of her was almost too much to bear. But I had to hold it together for both her and the children.

On the thirteenth day without the feeding tube, Gail wanted our youngest son, Richard, to spend the night by her side. I asked her, "Don't you want me to stay too?" But she indicated she did not, and I think it's because she knew that I'd already been with her day and night throughout this entire end stage ordeal, and that it would be good for me to go home and actually get some sleep.

So I went home, reluctantly, but glad for the chance to rest.

Richard sat with her all night, and he claims that he even got her to giggle once or twice while he was there. But it was obvious she was slipping away, and during the early morning hours he heard a terrible gasping sound that he learned later is called "the death rattle." It really scared him. He was 16 years old by then, and this was his first experience with death. He sat with her until the next afternoon, when I came to pick him up and take his place. I had no sooner gotten back home with him then the nursing home called to say come quickly: she was dying.

I raced back to the care facility and entered her room. She was making those strange gasping sounds again, and I could tell this was it. It was very scary watching her body go through its final changes, especially when I looked at her fingertips and saw they were turning blue. That's when reality sank in and I knew that death was near.

I suddenly had an eerie feeling. How on earth was I going to get through this ordeal? How could I possibly go on without her? She had been the focus of my time and attention for so long.... Fortunately, two of my good friends joined me there that afternoon as soon as they heard, and I am so thankful for them both. My friend, David, is a former hospice minister, and he knew exactly what to say and do. I couldn't have faced it without him. And his wife, Carolyn, was also very supportive in all that we had been going through. It was like God had provided two angels.

While we were sitting there with her, waiting for the end, a nurse came in and said that Gail had to be turned. So we left the room and gathered in the hallway. We had been talking only a few minutes when I felt this cool breeze go straight through my body. I remember wondering what it was at the time because there were no doors open that could've allowed a draft. I didn't say anything to my friends, but I just knew something was wrong. Right then it came to me: my wife had left us. Not two minutes later the nurse came out of Gail's room and told us that she had just passed away.

I must confess that I entered her room reluctantly. I didn't want to see her dead, and I was scared even to look. When I saw her lying there, though, I immediately recalled a dream I'd had about her just the night before. In that dream she had been lying in exactly the same way, with everything in her room just like it was here. It was unnerving - as though my dream had been preparing me for this moment. I leaned over, kissed her softly on the forehead, and said, "Good-bye, Tweedy-bird. I love you." I then turned to my friend and broke down in uncontrollable sobbing.

After a little while I got myself together and my friend, David, said a few words on her behalf and committed her soul back to God. It was shortly after that, I think, that I told my friends that I knew right when Gail died. I told them what I had experienced while we had been talking outside of her room, when that breeze blew right through me. When they heard me say that, they both exclaimed, right at the same time, "I did too!" They had each evidently felt the same thing but hadn't said anything about it either - to me or to each other. (Otherwise their response would've been, "We did too.") I realize that some of you might not believe me on this point, but that's okay. All I know is that all three of us, independently, felt something pass through our bodies at the same time.

There is one thing that can for sure be said about the spiritual realm: One never knows what may happen in situations like this! I know in my heart that my wife was saying good- bye to me when I felt that breeze pass through. Gail died June 30, 2003 eight days before her 46th birthday and twelve days before our 17th anniversary. Epilogue

In short, there were two funerals held for Gail: one here in Portland and one in Detroit, Michigan, where she is buried. The Portland funeral was held July 5th, and everything went as well as could be expected. A lot of Gail's friends and all my family were there, from as far away as California and Seattle. None of Gail's family from Detroit came, though - which is understandable: They were waiting for her to be shipped back to Michigan for burial.

The funeral here at home was very nice, and people said a lot of kind things about both Gail and me. But I was fragile and exhausted. As much as I tried to hold back the tears, whenever anyone mentioned Gail's name I started weeping. I could hardly talk to any of the well-wishers because I was so emotional. Richard, our youngest son, held up a lot better. In fact, he later told me that he found it difficult to cry at the time. He doesn't know why. Instead, the tears came several years later, when the realization of all that he had lost finally sunk in. His had hardly been a normal childhood, after all, spending so much time in a care home watching his mother lose her motor skills even as he was developing his.

After the Portland funeral, I flew Gail's body back to Detroit, along with Richard and myself. Everything was beautifully prepared by the time we arrived. There was a wake before the service began, which more than a thousand people attended, dropping by to pay their respects to the family. Gail's family is especially well known in that part of the country because of their close involvement with the musician Fred Hammond, who is famous all over the world for his urban gospel sound. He was Gail's brother-in-law and, together with her brother, Keith Staten, had formed a gospel band in the Staten family basement years ago, called "Commissioned." Fred was now a celebrity, and many Detroit police officers knew and respected him. They also knew that Gail was his sister-in-law. So they all got together and volunteered their time to escort the funeral procession and help control traffic, which was deeply appreciated by all of us.

Our middle son, Brian, bravely attempted to sing one of Gail's favorite hymns during the service: "It Is Well With My Soul." But it wasn't easy for him. He stopped part way through, overcome with emotion, then managed to pull himself together enough to finish the song. There was hardly a dry eye in the place, for most of us knew that Gail loved that song, and it meant even more in light of how much and how long she had suffered. Her soul truly had been well, despite the plight of her body. There is no doubt that it was GOD who had shepherded us through her fiery ordeal.

Upon returning to Portland a few days after the service, though, / felt utterly devastated. My whole life had revolved around caring for Gail, and now that she was gone my life seemed empty. I was totally and completely bereft. I found myself crying at odd times, for no apparent reason, and I couldn't seem to help it. So I called my mom, who lives down in Rome, Georgia, and she comforted me by reminding me that this was a necessary part of the mourning process. "Will I ever feel happy again?" I asked her. "I hate feeling this way!"

She assured me that I would eventually feel better, but that it could take a couple of years. "Oh my," I thought. "I'll never survive feeling this way that long!" And at times I thought I wouldn't. The depression got so bad I actually began hearing music in my head when I woke up most mornings, and sometimes at night, too. I didn't know how to stop it and began to think I was going "cuckoo." Dirty dishes began piling up in the kitchen sink, and my brothers (with whom I had been living since my return from Detroit) knew something was really wrong. I was normally the one who kept everything clean around the house I now shared with them. It took months before I began to rally, and I praise God for sending just the right people into my life at just the right time to help me through this long period of grief. That's another book in itself!

Several years after Gail's death, though, it felt like deju vu when I read about this woman, Terry Schiavo, who made national headline news. Her husband was going through the same thing I had gone through with his parents-in-law. Our local newspaper got wind that I had undergone a similar situation and asked to interview me. I did the interview and the next day ended up on the front page of The Oregonian. The local TV media read the newspaper article and decided they wanted to interview me as well. So I completed that interview and ended up on TV! Another television station (TBN: Trinity Broadcasting Network) saw me on TV and asked if they could film me for a 20-minute segment of their show, which they did.

All of this attention, however, was bringing back memories and emotions that I wasn't certain I wanted to deal with. I had already remarried by then, and I didn't want to bring this commotion into my current marriage. Thank God, my new wife, Maxine, is very understanding, and she encouraged me to air my views about this whole ordeal. My experiences were evidently useful and informative, for I received a lot of positive feedback from the community in response to those interviews.

I want to go on record, though, as saying there is a big difference between Terry Schiavo's case and Gail's. Terry had no written directive -- plus she had brain damage. Even if she had been able to communicate, she would not necessarily have been considered "fit" to assess her own situation. In retrospect, she would not have been in the national spotlight if her family knew for sure what her wishes were (via writing or some other form of lucid communication). At least my Gail had a written directive - which she then went against in order to please her parents, initially accepting a feeding tube she would later reject. I praise God she didn't have any brain damage and that she could still communicate by way of blinking her eyes. That (admittedly limited) form of communicating worked quite well, considering.

- So I would like to end this book with an expanded version of the advice I gave at the beginning as well as a summation of what our experiences taught me:

- Be sure to get a written directive or find out what your loved ones' wishes are before they are totally unable to respond!

- Develop some sort of distinctive nonverbal signal and/or "code" that both you and your loved one understand and agree upon in case they lose their ability to speak or write.

- Have a trusted witness on hand who sees what agreements have been made and who can then help arbitrate if disputes arise later on.

- Treat your loved one with the same consideration and respect you would if they still had all their faculties. Just because they can no longer respond doesn't mean they don't understand what's going on.

- Deeply consider your marriage vows before making them! The words, "In sickness and in health; 'til death do us part," take on a whole new meaning once tragedy strikes.

- Take time out to nourish yourself as a care-giver. The stress of caring for a loved one, even if they are in a nursing facility, can break your own health if you aren't careful.

- Don't give in to self-pity. There are always others who have it worse, and no one ever promised that life would be fair.

- Stay committed to God and your vows. He will give you the strength you need to face each day, one problem at a time!

www.ingramcontent.com/pod-product-compliance
Lightning Source LLC
Chambersburg PA
CBHW041629140626
46547CB00031B/1894